1st Recital Series

FOR OBOE

Including works of:
- James Curnow
- Craig Alan
- Douglas Court
- Mike Hannickel
- Timothy Johnson
- Ann Lindsay

Solos for Beginning
through Early Intermediate
level musicians

CURNOW®
MUSIC

EXCLUSIVELY DISTRIBUTED BY

HAL•LEONARD®
CORPORATION

7777 W. BLUEMOUND RD. P.O. BOX 13819 MILWAUKEE, WI 53213

Edition Number: CMP 0759.02

1st Recital Series
Solos for Beginning through Early Intermediate level musicians
Oboe

ISBN: 90-431-1746-3

CD Accompaniment tracks performed by Becky Shaw

CD number: 19.029-3 CMP

Foreword

High quality solo/recital literature that is appropriate for performers playing at the Beginner through Early Intermediate skill levels is finally here! Each of the **1st RECITAL SERIES** books is loaded with exciting and varied solo pieces that have been masterfully composed or arranged for your instrument.

Included with the solo book is a professionally recorded CD that demonstrates each piece. Use these examples to help develop proper performance practices. There is also a recording of the accompaniment alone that can be used for performance (and rehearsal) when a live accompanist is not available. A separate Piano Accompaniment book is available [edition nr. CMP 0760.02].

Table of Contents

☐   *Solo with accompaniment*

▨   *Accompaniment*

Track

2 **3** OBOE

Ludwig van Beethoven
1. ODE TO JOY
Arr. **Timothy Johnson** (ASCAP)

2. SKATER'S WALTZ

Douglas Court (ASCAP)

3. CRABAPPLE CROSSING

Ann Lindsay (ASCAP)

5. AUTUMN LEAVES

for Kristen

Douglas Court (ASCAP)

Johannes Brahms
6. HUNGARIAN DANCE # 5

Arr. **James Curnow** (ASCAP)

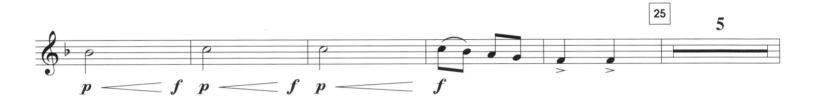

7. PROCESSION OF HONOR

Timothy Johnson (ASCAP)

Victor Herbert
Fantasy On
8. DAGGER DANCE
from "NATOMA"

Arr. **Craig Alan** (ASCAP)

9. RONDO

Timothy Johnson (ASCAP)

10. THE RED BALLOON

James Curnow (ASCAP)

Moderately fast with feeling (♩ = 100)

14   Copyright © 2002 by Curnow Music Press, Inc.

11. IN A FRENCH CAFE

Mike Hannickel (ASCAP)

Quickly and happily (♩ = 108)

Georges Bizet
12. HABANERA
from
Carmen

Arr. **James Curnow** (ASCAP)

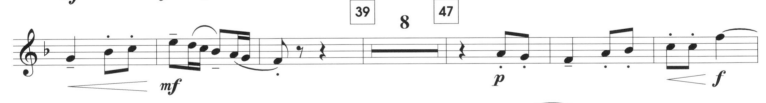